Especially for Adults

11 Intermediate Piano Solos for Older Students

Dennis Alexander

M000086875

Over the years, my work with adult piano students has proven to be immensely rewarding and gratifying. Adults tend to be very self-motivated individuals who study piano because they love music and have always wanted to play piano, or in many cases, regret quitting piano lessons as a child. Their musical interests are different from those of children taking piano lessons. Adults need music that "warms the heart," provides opportunity for gradual technical growth and provides motivation for consistent practice.

The music in *Especially for Adults*, Book 2 is designed to accomplish all of the above. Adults will experience a real sense of accomplishment when they play these solos that contain beautiful, rich harmonies; numerous patterns that easily fit the hands and lyrical melodies that speak to their emotions. The pieces sound sophisticated and the titles themselves reflect this sophistication. In addition to the original music composed for this series, I have also arranged some favorite classical melodies that adults will know and enjoy.

The *Especially for Adults* series is the perfect supplement for any adult method book and will provide motivational repertoire in a variety of appealing styles for teenagers and adults of all ages. Enjoy!

Dennis Alexander

Alfred

Starbeams

Dennis Alexander

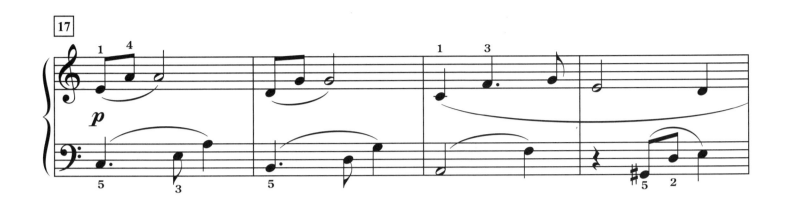

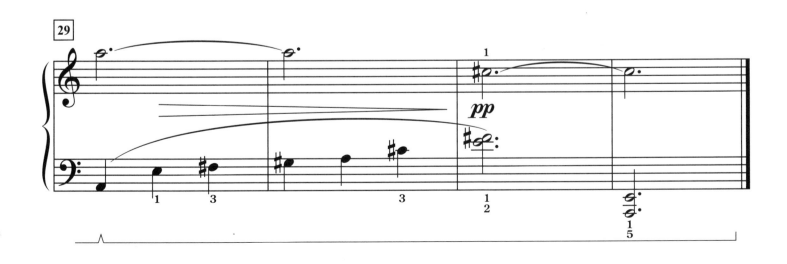

Theme from the 2nd Movement
Sonata Pathétique

Ludwig van Beethoven (1770–1827)
Op. 13
Arranged by Dennis Alexander

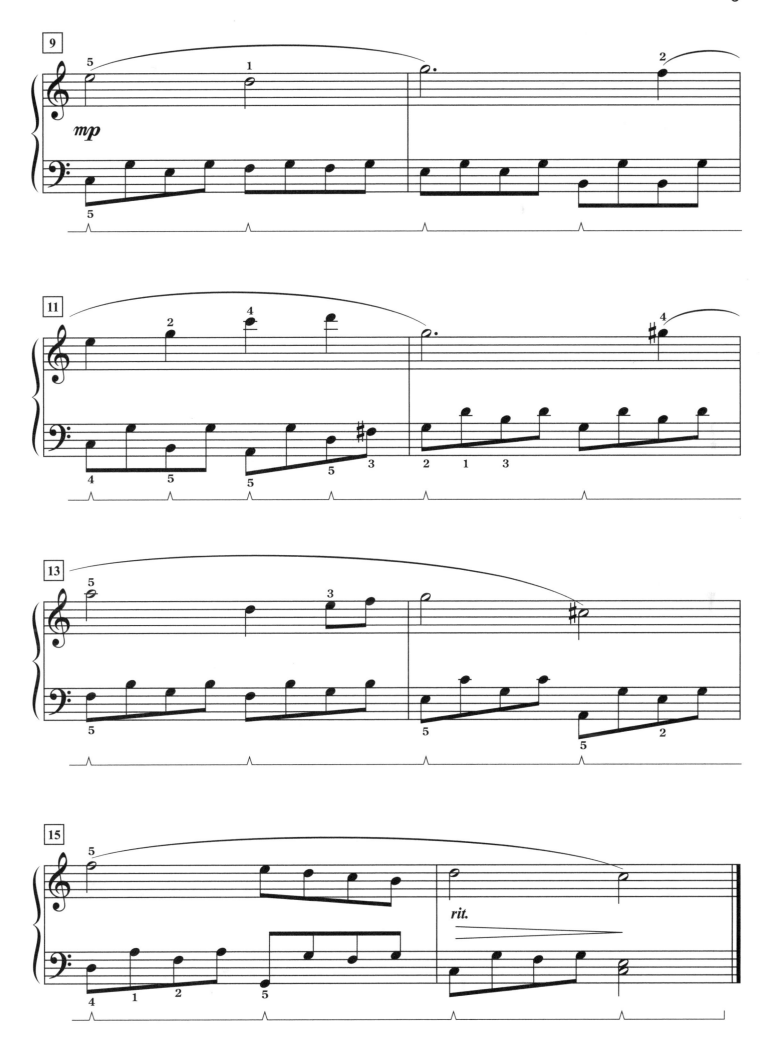

Lots o' Blues

Dennis Alexander

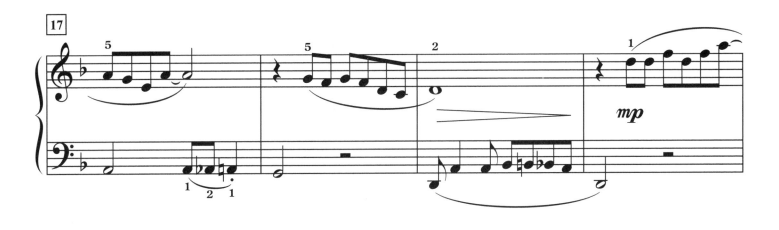

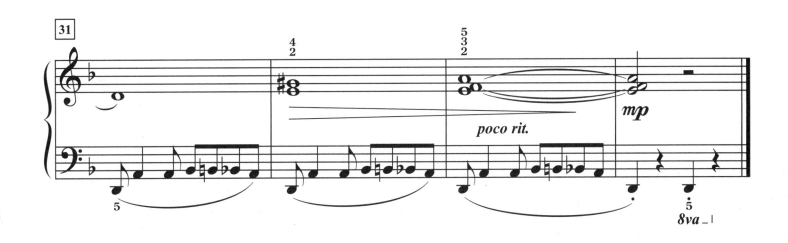

8va

for Bill

Thinking of You

Dennis Alexander

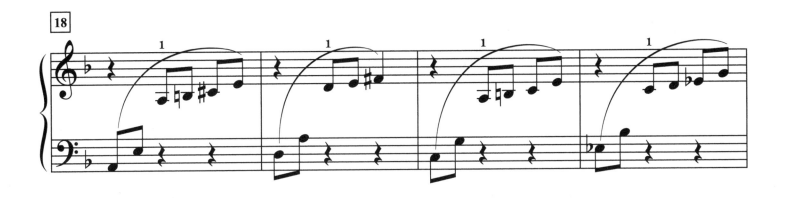

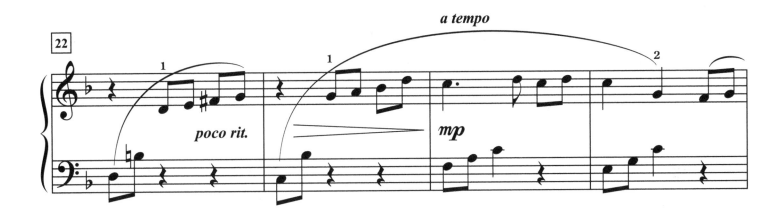

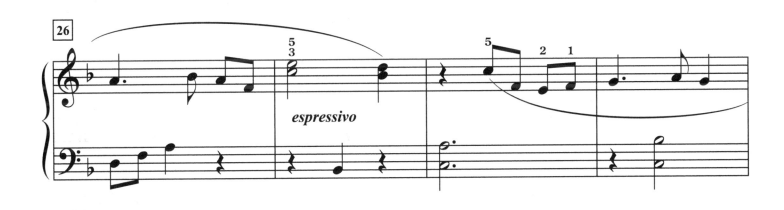

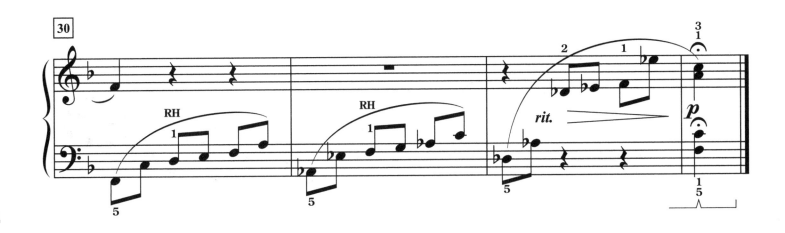

Downtown Boogie

Dennis Alexander

Danny Boy
(Londonderry Air)

Irish Folk Song
Arranged by Dennis Alexander

Simple Gifts

Shaker Melody
Arranged by Dennis Alexander

Midnight Rag

Dennis Alexander

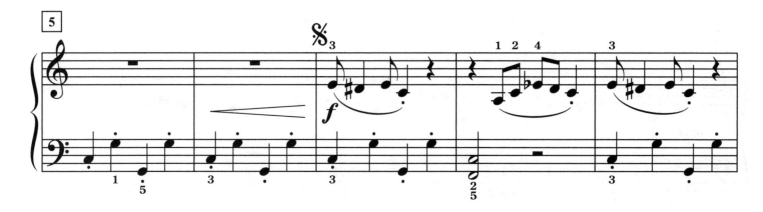

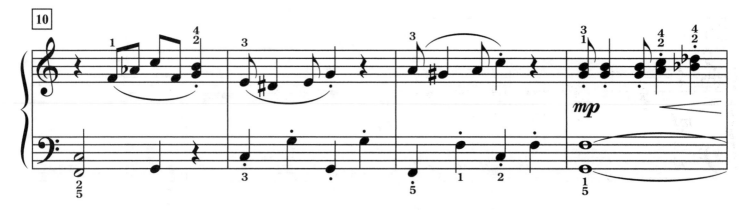

Song without Words

Dennis Alexander

Valsette

Dennis Alexander

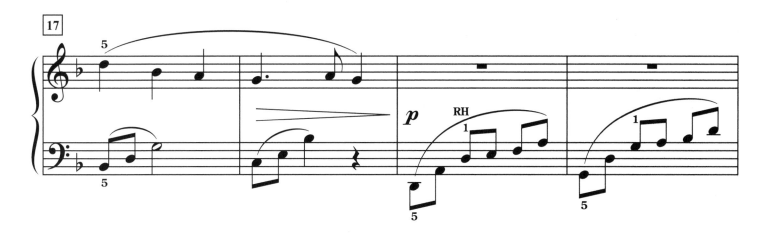

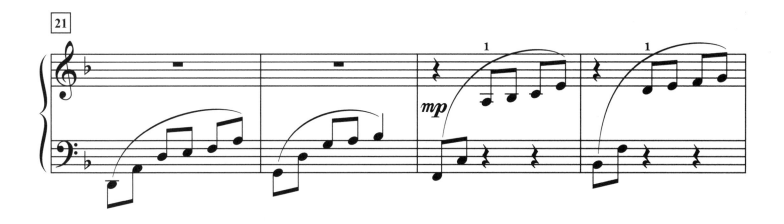

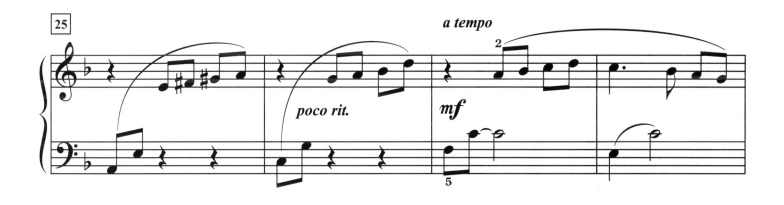

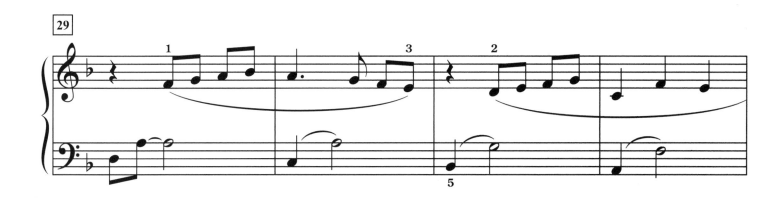

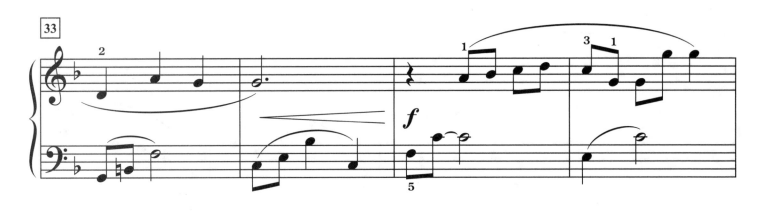

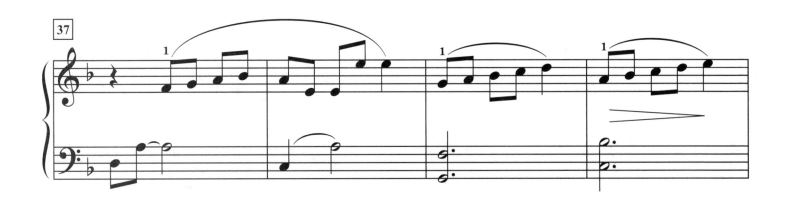

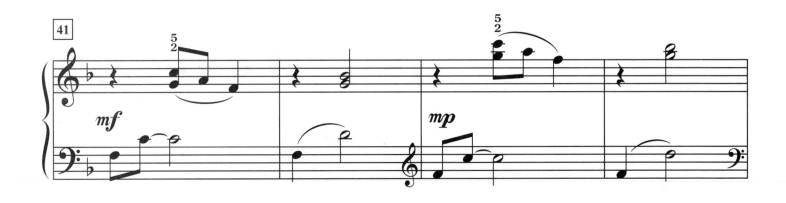

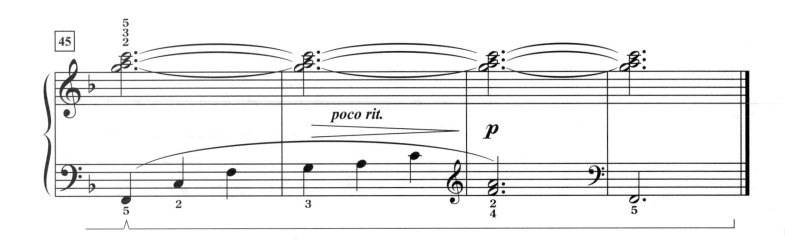

Distant Memories

Dennis Alexander